MW01113563

Watermark

Poems by Elisabeth Stoner
Photographs by April Allyson Abel

For Barbarana
and
Katherine
with love
from Elisabeth

For Dick and Joel

ALL RIGHTS RESERVED
COPYRIGHT © 2016

ISBN: 978-1-61422-832-5

Watermark

Written by: Elisabeth Stoner

Printed in Collierville, TN USA
InstantPublisher.com, Inc.

No part of this publication may be reproduced or transmitted in any form or by any means, electronically or mechanically, including photocopy, recording, or any information storage and retrieval system, without permission in writing to the Publisher.

Table of Contents

The Formula

Follow winter's
Unfisting amaryllis:
Burst to stripes
Pink, white.
Just add water,
Add light.

Great Blue---Spring

We emerge from the pine grove's
fallen logs and dappled winter shadows---
arriving at this tiny weathered dock
that gives onto a lighter, open view.

This pond has been---till recently---black water---
Now, water lilies carpet it---
joining grasses and sedges---cat-tails,
heart-leaved pickerel---lacey algaes.

Bull frogs do their fog horns.
Dozing turtles might be bronze or stone.
That water snake is probably not a copperhead.
Out there, what seems to be a tall stick---
or a pole, upright in the distance---

in one breath, blooms and unfurls,
hurling itself into a whirring sky-high uplift
that circles above our little world
like a feathered god.

Great Blue---Fall

At the far end of this down-hill, wooded path
is another pond---even smaller than the last.
Backwater, black water,
narrowed now by encroaching deadwood falling,
sassafras and alder hanging over, reaching,
blown-out cattails dropping fluffy froth,
clumps of grasses crowding.

A slender, torch-like tree,
still hung with twirling, golden pieces---
uprooted now, keeled over, slanting down
face-to-face with its own reflections---
dissolving, sinking pages, mottled, stained---
once-bright colors disintegrating.

This pond, already small---now smaller.
Too small to accommodate any super-being---
Too tight, too confining to allow
for the wonder of ascension.

Yet---here it is---or was---or really is---
Silent, stalk-like, invisible---
that primordial airborne mystery---
roaring aloft---soaring---its wingspan greater than any pond---
any ocean---any heaven.

New Moon Tide

New moon, high tide---
the gray-jade ocean heaves---
surging and slamming the shore.

We walk the wrack line,
reading the leavings of last night's havoc---
ripped seaweed, shattered shells, ravaged marine debris.

Our perilous way along the edge of the surf narrows---
lunging waves thunder higher and closer,
licking and biting out the remaining dune---
despite the spartina grass planted there to secure the wall---
despite the roots of previous trees---
now protruding like cut cords.

Single file we must go now---
aiming for the safety of the jetty at the Point
and the path that rises up from there.

The guide reaches out for me---
holds on---lets go---and calls out,
"Sir! Could you help *her* along?"

A fragrance of a memory slips in,
reviving the sensations
of a past occasion of such mindful stepping.
That time---at the top
of the cloud-high ridge of Waimea Canyon---
with sheer drops straight down---on both sides----over rocks---
down to a different, distant sea.

Now, once again, I am delivered
by hands I may not be aware of----
hands that boost me---lift me---release me---
according to a plan
too perfect for me to understand.

Ought to Repot

Why cannot my house plants
Stay in the pot in which
I bought them?

I adopted them because they bloomed,
And now, too soon,
They drool leaves---bloomless frauds!

I have sought an orphanage for bloomless plants,
But there are not a lot.
Perhaps that bore next door
Will take one or two.

Okay, I'll root a few,
And squatting, repot some, too.
I know I ought to do it.

Peridot

I dreamed a ruin
Of crumbled stone, four sides
Weatherbeaten, open to the sky,
With a peaked wall at one end
Where the altar must have stood.

The dream voice showed me
Bright green grass
Where life shimmered
Iridescent in chilly fall.
The grass gleamed wet
In the square outlined by broken walls.

I remembered another broken house
Jammed in sumac, down by the train.
Cement block that structure was.
But I took it for a chapel---
By its dazzling stained-glass window
Miraculously intact,
Still shining on the rubble.

As I came closer, the window shifted:
Its leading outlines branching,
Changing lucent planes of peridot and ruby,
And igniting shards of flame.

The October sun
Glazed the leaves and twigs
Beyond that frame. No glass at all.
These trees still stand like candles:
Exalting ruins into chapels
And greening the grass of fall.

Receive Yourself

Receive yourself the way you are today,
and even if it takes audacity,
renew yourself whatever comes your way.

Plant your feet in the sucking surge. Outstay
the undertow of past authority:
receive yourself the way you are today.

You may be persuaded to overplay
your charms, but that's a sort of forgery.
Renew yourself whatever comes your way.

Does old unease cause strength to run away?
Defuse the depth charge of apology.
Receive yourself the way you are today.

The east wind sings bright sun, black ice, salt spray.
Birds fly despite the ambiguity.
Renew yourself whatever comes your way.

You are a gleaming beacon. Don't betray
your light, your heart, your love, your majesty.
Receive yourself the way you are today.
Renew yourself whatever comes your way.

"Rehoboth to Pump Waste into the Ocean"

1. The Sea I Dream Of

Come, dive with me into the sea I dream of:
clear, translucent, aquamarine. Deeper---
dancing, glancing light brightens sapphire, cerulean.
Deeper still, glistening, iridescent beryl, emerald---finally,
vivid turquoise, currents of cobalt, purple, darkening black.
Caverns, crevasses, shelves, plates, tunnels, pelagic ledges,
deepest caves---native structures within the pure,
mysterious, mystical, primeval living waters of the deep.

Remains of ancient civilizations: a sunken, armless statue,
a broken ship, its master now a leering, waving skeleton,
scattered flatware, a treasure chest now empty,
except for a family of fish making it their home.
Fractured marble porticos, peristyles, colonnades---
graceful wrecks from other vainglorious eras.

Beams of light: my ocean teeming, full of life.
We see in the forests of the sea: seaweeds, grasses,
phytoplankton, sea anemones, water hyacinth—
bunches of sargassum—-laughing dolphins use it as a toy—
tossing it to pals, wearing as adornment,
rolling over, flapping tails in unison,
chirping, clicking, whistling back and forth.

Dusky dolphins herd anchovies, take turns gulping.
We see rays, sharks, eels, tuna, perch, sea turtles, seals,
a whale, horseshoe crabs, rock fish, oysters, squid,
coral, octopus, a team of porpoises----maybe a manatee.

2. Today

We see killer plastic bags resembling delicious jelly fish,
water bottles breaking down, mistaken for food, too.
Gyres of trash. Oil spills. Dredging.
Drilling's raucous racket halts echo location, navigation,
makes marine mammals crazy.
Almost every day, we find another carcass on our beach.

The outfall will pump into our ocean
pharmaceuticals, hormones, heavy metals, pain killers, antibiotics,
birth-control and tranquilizing drugs, nitrogen, phosphorus...
Think of the effect on life and habitat.

"Last year we saw a 500% increase in dolphin deaths.
The situation is already perilous.
If the outfall is built, the nightmare
will never end."

3. Act

But these are only paper words---thrown out in tomorrow's trash.
Come, stand with us in the shallows as we support
a dying dolphin so it does not drown.

Come, stand with us at the steel table as the 10 blade
cuts into the once-luminescent, now dull carcass,
revealing parasites, poisons—perhaps a cancer, an embryo?

Come, help us count the dolphins before they are no more.

Come, help us restore our gorgeous ocean.

Parable of the Lighted Truck

I wish, when my father lay dying,
that I'd reminded him of the time when
we followed the truck down the mountain.

He'd been worrying because some cousin had scared him
with her shaky notions of the afterlife—
really with her own fears about dying.

I wish I'd asked my father, Do you remember that trip…?
and he'd eagerly look at me in his alert way.
(At the end, he suddenly remembered all kinds of things.)

Remember when we were driving home over the Alleghenies
in the old Chevy, pushing later into the night
than we'd meant to or than was at all sensible,

when a sudden snowstorm blew up, almost a white-out?
(I also wish that I'd told him how much I loved
that bright green duvetyn coat I was wearing back then.)

A half-century later, I still feel the touch of its soft hand,
the round of its covered buttons, the slick of its satin lining.
I'd fallen in love with the coat in a shop in Petosky,

and even though it was not in the budget, he'd allowed it.
A coat can be like a house or a belief--- a safe place to be
when you feel unease about where the road may be leading you.

Anyway, when he asked me did I think death happened the way
that foolish person had said, I wish I'd reminded him of how
when the night was getting later and he was trying to steer

us safely along the edges of the sheer drop-offs,
not really seeing in the low clouds and the snow falling—
how the arbor vitae truck had materialized in front of us,

tail lights blazing—its whole hull studded
with running lights—outlining its cargo of evergreens
riding unshakably, making perhaps for some placid farm.

The truck headed steadily right—down the ramp
at the New Bedford exit. Not knowing where we were going,
we followed the light until we beheld
a sign saying Welcome to the New Bedford Inn. Lamps shone
in each window. Inside, hot baths, white sheets,
and a boundless sense of wild security.

On Being Two Places at Once

Occupying the forwarding address,
Prior to departing the old home base,
I was coexisting geographically, synchronizing space.
(A simultaneous bi-location at a schizo-place.)
Time warps are fun for arriving before you leave.
What I did (you know what I mean)
Was to temporarily split the scene.

Old-Stuff Ghazal

His turnout---disarray! So long
A phase. He's been blasé so long.

His stuff's old. Nothing's up-to-date.
He's had that Chevrolet so long.

No fashion sense at all, alas.
His wardrobe's been passé so long.

His grooming is not up-to-snuff—
His hair hangs lank and gray—so long.

Maybe he'll ask her for a date—
Send a communiqué so long—

Detailing his plans to play croquet,
view etchings on display so long.

Of course, she wants to be polite.
Says she can only stay so long.

She's through with couplets—any kind—
It's late, she's tired, she'll say, So long!

Grandson Summer---Passing Through

We rarely see each other---
Georgian Bay, L.A., Peru, Boston, Duke, Bellevue--------Milford.
Yet, miraculously, this summer, both grandsons passed through here.

We first met at another time of passing through---
Our elders had been summoned up their golden tunnels to heaven,
and these fresh-minted baby beings were being pushed down theirs.
I attended all these goings and comings.
I still have dresses, scarves from those days.

Even though three times a mother----to me these fragile, tiny,
half-blind, seemingly semi-amphibious babes were daunting .
I hesitated to touch, to hug, to help---for fear of hurting.

Now, these smiling giants offer muscled arms so I don't fall---
do the dishes, strip their bed, fix the computer, open doors ,
carry my 10-ton backpack, laugh at my jokes, keep me safe.
Two of my feet fit into one of their boat-like flip–flops.

Now they are gone---on their way---one to write a computer language
beyond my understanding, wearing a red backwards baseball cap,
black earring, beard---maybe away in a foreign land.

The other, saving lives in a wild hospital emergency room,
listening to, singing songs with sick, dying, destitute crazies---
then writing science—and loving it.

I cannot see their wings, but I do see these grandsons flying---
as are we all---finding our way together or alone
as we pass through.

Origin of the word gazpacho: a Mazarab word meaning residue or fragments

How to Make Gazpacho

In blistering August sun, visit Sue's garden
where the guardian tall poplar trees whisper
that they will long outlive us foolish humans.

Fill your basket with crazy tomatoes---fat heirlooms,
red and yellow striped---one pink with a bluish cheek, purple inside.
Pillars of wintered-over Swiss chard stand sentinel---
weathered, protective, edible.

Pull a sweet onion or two, and whatever else says, "Take me."
Maybe a cucumber, some garlic, even a melon.
This garden may seem wild. It is---wild and wise.

Back in your kitchen, chop up whatever comes to mind---
that jerk at Comcast---chop faster---garlic and tomatoes, of course---
men who call me, "young lady," my balky computer---cucumber,
celery, bits of melon---with grated daikon radish, if you dare.
Add background notes of sherry vinegar, olive oil, salt from the sea air,
a pinch of cayenne in memory of that mild flirtation.
Make a chiffanade of fresh basil for your later presentation.

Gently fold in ghosts of long-gone summers---
gin & tonics at the yacht club,
ravishing glances, that fitted Liberty Lawn sundress---
saxophone show tunes wafting through French doors opening
onto the moon-struck golf green where we hesitated,
lingering---unmoored---all at sea in the smell of the new-mown grass.

Light your white beeswax candles.
Place a jug of zinnias, golden rod, cilantro.
Bless your luscious bowl of summertime.
Sing an incantation:
"Lovely living food, sanctify us all."

My New Stepping Stone
for Celeste

Recently, my steps have been faltering, wobbling, stopped.

Then, beneath the trees------I see mosaics
Shards of vessels----crocks, bottles, goblets-------
Perhaps a shattered chalice-----------
Also, flat glass scrap, as if from stained-glass windows------
Placed with fragments of broken mirrors.

Bits of past existences------dismantled, smashed-----
Now reset in cement as garden ornaments.

I take home one stepping stone-------
Now half-hidden amid my fruiting blueberries,
Flowering jasmine, geranium, rose.

My new stepping stone sparkles as I place my foot.

Sacred Studies

The small circle of lamplight, the desk chair, the fur breathing-and-purring machine, the oak table, the dream book, the I Ching, the stack of poems on the floor, a jar of daffodils, olive oil on greens and garlic, local strawberries, the growing grass, the small circle of lamplight.

Sea Anemones

Sans mask, sans snorkel,
I sank in the transparent sea
To twice the height of a man.

Body drowned, breathing easily,
With single-eyed seeing, I
Hung in gelatinous washes,
Wafting like lashes
Of fringed civilizations
Concealed
In grottos carved out of light.

Dioramas with candles,
Guarded by urchins
Showed the sets for
The next decade's drama.

Sea Change

Friends now, surely an upward step,
We tread Sunday evening's back road
Where last night's storm tore through,
Drenching a plausible fire.
Muddy water rushed in gullies,
Washing runnels wet as potter's slip.
Arm in arm now, not embracing
We falter on sandal-cutting rocks,
Dreading friendship's higher rarity.

The surging tidal wave of corn
Whispers her fertile roar. Towering
Stalks livened by new rain
Suggest a dance down flapping banners.
One beacon evening star---the answer to
That first-lighted farmhouse lantern
Beckoning over oceanic fields.

Sea Chantey

Pin my heart on a rock to dry.
Wipe soft cotton on a Blue Cross sky.
Sand storms, blast my doldrums away---
Shine my halo with clean salt spray.

Gong rings the buoy, la lee, la lay.

Cauterize the rift with the sun's hot glint.
Bind up the split with a driftwood splint.
Wash out the wound with the green salt sea
And heal the gash that's me and thee.

Gong rings the buoy, la lay, la lee.

In the Ring

A man who said he'd always love me leaves his voice on my
machine. Ten years it's been---I'm quite revised. Still glib, he
erases continents and time, purring, "I'd love to see
you, dear---I'm flying in from Singapore." I can't deny
I'm fascinated. What's his game? What to wear? Will he try
to revive some dormant need, trampling over past debris?
Can I hold him off with devastating civility?
How to deflect his nosy questions? (He's going to pry.)
By screening all my calls, I side-step any need to chat.
He tries, hangs up---frequently---believing he's concealing
his muzzled raging bellow. More calls at all hours. His last
ring comes at midnight. Passive, I sit listening to that
familiar voice booming in my room. He's stymied, wheeling;
I feel the pent-up fury of the beast as he pounds past.

The Non-Pick-Up

Again, he leaves his voice on my machine,
Saying he is missing dear old friends.
For one, I'm never old---I feel sixteen---
And I'm not sure that we were ever friends.
He does not mention any ETA,
Much less suggest some dates when he'd be free.
He doesn't say where he intends to stay.
Could it be he plans to mooch in on me?
Does he call at dawn to trap me off-guard?
Or because his hostess is still asleep?
(Finagling, he believes we're easy marks.)
Still glib, he offers no way I can reach
him, while sourly lamenting his bad luck.
Good luck can be made. I simply don't pick up.

Seasoning

Traveling home by night,
I see across the fields
Huge headlights beaming.
Some epic creature or machine
Proceeds through lakes of hay,
Snatching up wave
After wave and baling it.

The peaches are over.
Wild geese fly earlier this year.
A tea rose unfurls her spice.

I slow dance, alone and never alone.
You stand ahead of me, waiting.
Cold in my summer clothes,
I consider how my light is spent.
Listening to the owls,
I stand at the stove
Waiting for the water to boil.

We are part of the stars.

Souls in Shells

Among the cobalt
Pyramidal pillars
Of submerged Atlantis,
They hang in blue flotillas
And they aestivate in shoals.
The fluvial streams
Of the circular succession
Sweep them higher to oceanic pools.

Souls in shells
Impelled upon their separate trajectories
By predetermined tides---
Subjects of the sunrise
And minions of the moon,
Internal timings guide them
To their forecast rendezvous.
Riding final froth, they're
Paired in the estuary,
Orbiting their shallow pool
Till succeeding tides excuse them
From that provisional school. And then
The current tows them under
And sucks them out to sea again.

Stealing Chihuly

The gallery was a receptacle of darkness—
except for tiny ceiling spotlights
that ignited island-like displays
of what some say
are blown-in-the-moment
eddies of frozen fire.

Like Prometheus, who stole fire from Olympus
by hiding it in the hollow
of a fennel reed,
I shadowed in obliquely
and let my costumed solar plexus swallow
a single star of that guarded galaxy.

Don't tell. For now,
I'm pregnant, alive
with dreadful, fragile radiance.

Stepping Back

We ride over back roads to Yellow Springs.
Sunshine gleams on queen's lace, tiger lilies, hayfields.
Cows cluster under willows by a stream.

Memories of old towns—Hudson, Easton, Hamilton—
locales like Shelter Island, Fisherman's Paradise,
where wooden houses have shutters that close,
and lattice covers dark spaces beneath slanting porches.

In those days, cooking smells floated:
Gooseberry pies oozing with juices,
berries the children had hand-picked that morning,
pot roast with horseradish fresh from the garden,
real mashed potatoes, buttermilk biscuits
patted out by strong kitchen women.

I'd bathe and put on my cross-bar dotted swiss for dinner.
In the dusky evening we'd walk out
under the heavy-leaved trees for ice cream
churned from cow's cream mined with black bing cherries
that popped to the tooth.
Then, someone always knew what to do.

Here at Yellow Springs, I travel back again.
Early Sunday morning, the crafts festival is dewy fresh.
We walk through an ultramarine tunnel.
Sassafras, swamp maple, tulip poplar, white pine—
tree leaves glimmering and glinting all around us
like a passage through a sheltering sea,
translucent, healing, green, leading to the sunny meadow.

Potters and weavers smile out from their tents,
returning me to my Brownie days at Camp Butterworth.
A smith pounds his glowing iron figures
beneath a spreading buckeye tree abloom with candles.
A farm woman ladles cold lemonade
from a bucket with ice and lemon slices floating inside it.

The smell of meat cooking over charcoal draws us.
From our lunch table on the slanting porch
we view a walled garden. Wet black mossy rocks
surround sweet william, lemon lily, delphinium, geranium,
coreopsis, poppy, bluebell, hollyhock, forget-me-not.

In the shade of our straw hats,
we climb to the rim of the fieldstone hospital ruin,
now filled with a garden of medicinal herbs.
Lovage, lavender, fennel, bee balm.
A memorial to dead soldiers,
whose ancient pain lies silent and buried
in unmarked graves under these flowery fields.

The Coast Is Clear

He telephones his lady friend,
"Is the coast clear?"
It is, indeed. They meet.
She drives them out to experience the radiant fall.
They ride through Spring Grove Cemetery,
Where mates and mutual memories rest in labeled spaces.
"We live under the same roof,"
They tell inquirers with gentle smiles.
"We eat Graeter's vanilla ice cream at 9:00 p.m., just us."

In April, for her birthday,
He plans fresh lilies-of-the-valley flown from Holland.
An armload of lilacs arrives after their latest ride.
He, stretched out in the ambulance; she at his side,
Traveling towards one more invasive procedure at the hospital.
"A fun day, overall," he says.

When asked where he will journey when unhooked from tubes,
He dreams of the canals of Holland—
An easy drift past windmills.
She has agreed to come along.
But, he states with vigor,
As always, they will sleep in separate rooms!
Is this emphasis perhaps intended as an example
For a sometimes-seen-as-straying daughter?
As added final words of fatherly advice?

Just as he seems to glide backward, to recede into graying mist,
He rebounds with energy, pronouncing lists:
"Always keep a little cash on the side."
"Read the Wall Street Journal."
"Drive like the other guy is nuts."
"Is there anything else we should talk about?"

Here is a man I never knew,
Who hid four live turkeys in the cellar as a boy,
Who sang songs in a contest at the nickel show.
Whose fishing worms vanished, a warning to leave the mountains.

We knew about the Salvage Corps,
But the Salvage Corps cannot respond forever.
Tendrils running rooted underground knit up.
Gradually, methodically,
He becomes eligible for the turn,
Into time beyond space beyond time,
And the coast is clear.

The Dig

Mica bits blew away in the air,
Micro chips of glittery lives
Flying away in the dry dust
Of the first layers of sand
Unearthing the hard-packed strata.

Finger-tips scratch through grit
Given to cave-ins and underground rivers,
Nails bleeding on broken shells
And breaking at rocks,
Not seeking the mere light of China,
But grasping for
That hand.

Action At the Ball Park

giddy girls with iPhones
gobble sloppy hot-dogs
preen and pose for selfies
click and fidget snapshot

we spot a skidding get
magic--- just caught the line
pinch-hitter safe at home
speedy guy steals second

Day Lily

burning bright
bud to flare
day to night
took it to the limit
one last time
beat the heat
late july

The Mean

A glassine tarpaulin's stretched taut
Over the yeasty sea
Whereunder flights of fishies
Pulse in dashes and
Carp glide serenely
In their circuits
Like oblate oranges.

On the encasing bubble cover
I stand, then walk, balancing,
Alone as wind.
The sun below shines up
To the one wired in a porcelain sky.

Traveling

I'd expected it to be an easy path
through palm trees and orchids,
just a gentle hike
over the hilly trails of Kauai.

My little knit dress and sandals seemed correct.
I hand-carried my things in a string bag,
surely no need for a backpack.
It was just a stroll.

But soon, the travel became more serious.
Wet mud, on a steep slant,
oozed at my ankles.   I slipped
as we pulled ourselves
branch to branch along a stream,
through a wood of gullies and bogs.

Ahead, car-sized boulders in high grass
obscured the path—if there was one.
We inched along a narrow ledge
at the edge of a steep canyon drop-off,
eventually arriving at a waterfall
where others had already
hurled themselves into the sluice.

I sat frozen on a rock—knowing
I could have been killed or crippled
except for my intense planting of foot after foot,
and the woman who took my string bag out of my hand,
and the men who knew the precise second when
to extend a hand or to boost me from behind,
then vanish in silence till the next time.
His eyebrow told me I'd not be left alone for the hike back.
I felt passed on by hands seen and unseen
till we all returned to the edge of the preserve
where we'd started a long time ago—
in some distant, forgotten age.

They said I looked like a babe.
Shorn of all but my existence.
Just born, I dissolved.

My Coiffures

As a teen, I believed I resembled
(do you remember ?) Veronica Lake,
a wave dipping over my right eye---
which may have impeded
my vision---and invited judgment
from those who failed
to understand what a star
she was at that time.

A scrupulous page-boy, stiff with Aqua Net,
followed.   Then came Marilyn and Grace---
blond royalty with pin curls for me to mimic.

Next, my coif resembled a blooming spring dandelion---
a composite flower head---
Kodak yellow---like the sun.

Nowadays, my head appears to have gone to seed---
having matured into a ball of fluff, a white moon
awaiting a breath from the east wind
that will arrive in perfect time
to blow away the puff ball
releasing its tiny parachutes---
freeing all the seeds
which resemble stars.

My Clouds

Long ago, when I flew on Pan Am, all dressed up
in my hand-me-down Davidow suit, pearls,
pill box hat, high heels, white gloves---
friendly cloud banks outside the aircraft window
escorted me---- clouds like shape–shifting cream puffs, teddy bears,
Cary Grants, magnificent mountain peaks, billowing ball gowns......

Today, I sit on my tiny balcony in my new Gudrun frock,
spooning up vanilla ice cream, surrounded by clouds of white
blossoms---jasmine, geranium, gardenia, daisy, petunia, euphorbia,
white candle, phalaenopsis, cyclamen, peace lily, mandevilla.

Looking up at the sky, I see my old cloud friends still passing by.
Beclouded as I am by age, I recognize them in a new way:
Nowadays, my clouds have soft smiling faces---angels, maybe---
or demigods---nebulous yet welcoming,
vaporous shapes, shimmering white, back-lighted in gold.

Moving Ballast

Seasick, sailing my cockleshell
Into walls of liquid glass that
Swell and break, flooding the deck,
Washing my cargo of wind-eggs west.
I drench my cochineal dress
Bailing the bilge of scarlet tears,
I'm steadied to ride out the flooding blast
By a deadline tied to my toe at a price.
This gale's emotion is excessively wet,
But it's better than dry navigation on ice.

Lovely Latkes

The Fed Ex man kept
ringing insistently
until I made it to my door---
knowing he was bringing
to my East-coast kitchen
handmade potato pancakes
packed with melting ice.

Just hours ago in Los Angeles,
Joel had magically transformed
masses of hand-grated potatoes, onions,
scallions, parsley, eggs, secret seasonings---
into sautéed patties too exquisite
to be called mere pancakes.
A big box of tasty miracles for me.
No poor Manischewitz mix for him.

Now the latkes are safely mine.
Eagerly, in the stainless pan Joel also gave me,
I heat a few up to try---
biscuit-brown with crispy, lacy edges,
tender, slender centers.
Nutritious, too with all that potassium---
Curative for any qualm.

Now I'm feeling grounded, centered, calm.
I have a freezer full of lovely latkes
to solidly sustain me
with sour cream, pepper, salt,
through these dark and chilly, wet spring days
---and nights---
Savory sturdy food to bolster me
until I see the sun and son again.

Hugging Pantoum

It's like hugging a teacup, hugging you.
Bony shoulders, like bone china.
Angled handles hard to hold.
Eggshellish, but not like glass.

Bony shoulders, like bone china.
Lustreware, an iridescent glow.
You are eggshellish, but not like glass.
I don't think you'll break.

Lustreware, an iridescent glow.
A light that seems to come from gold.
I don't think you'll break.
You're homey, steady, more like a mug.

I have outstretched arms. I want to hug.
Still, your handles are hard to hold.
I'll be gentle with my embrace,
It is like hugging a teacup, hugging you.

Brief Takes on Time
for Lauren

I awake in the muddled dark. The clock says 5:35.
But is this day starting or ending?
Is it time to make breakfast or supper?
What day of the week might today be?

Chill dark has crept in beneath the blinds
where sunlight and sunlit ideas once glittered.
Now, any brilliance lies passively in a puddle of dusk.

Soon we must again change the time.
Changing time seems hubristic and dangerous.
Why say we are saving daylight?
Why pretend? No daylight has ever been saved.

In class, I ask, Is time going faster?
No, the universe is expanding.
In five billion years, our sun will disintegrate, says Jon.

Meanwhile, I'm cold.
Layering these heavy old clothes so they look happy
takes too much of my time.

Chinese medicine says fall is a fine, white time.
Crisp. Inspiration comes from above.
Clarity. What is no longer useful falls away.
A time of stark contrast.
Leafless trees against the autumn sky.
Ashes. Snow.

Even so, I'll call Stephen Hawking.
He will know.
Professor Hawking, Sir,
Where did summer go?

In the Driver's Seat

In those child-like clear days,
Our light beach-towel-capes billowed out.
We raced the sandpipers and were Supermen.

Enthroned, feet towards the sea,
Our father packed sand around us,
Fashioning intricate automobiles.
Wiggling our toes in the grit,
We drove magical cars then,
My brother and I.

Incursion

Off the train they came,
with a mobilized yard sale:
a stroller, a Pac-n-Play,
a Box-Bag loaded with Sippy Cups,
puzzles, Tupperware snack boxes,
story-books, diapers, Balmex,
car-cars, bears,
and the babies' babies.

They knocked over vases
onto the photographs,
and, when pressed,
said sorry or thank-you. They rolled
down the hill and rode on my tractor. They spilled
Juicy Juice onto the new upholstery.
Forgot about naps.
When told don't chase the cat,
they chased after the cat
just to see what would happen.
They behaved at the diner.
Stuck tongues out at the neighbors.
Exchanged stares with a 20-year-old tortoise.
They rode off in a flurry
of kisses and bye-byes,
leaving behind loose
Cheerios, sticky
handprints, crayoned love
notes, dead
dandelions, silence.

The Cure

The metal folding chairs are cold and hard.
The student next to me says Hi---her face
a fertile plain, expansive, yet recalling
my old friend who rashly took her leave,
leaving all her kids, cutting short her work.
The awful news came from her minister.

My new friend's husband is a minister.
She confides that sometimes her life is hard,
devoted to church-secretary work,
choir practice, teas, bazaars (she makes a face)---
an existence she often dreams of leaving
to follow her deepest heartfelt calling

to practice healing arts. She feels called
to advance her skills and minister
to the sick. Unpleasant to ask for leave;
her husband would be bound to take it hard.
She flounders, afraid she could not face
the fluster, the churn of the inner workings

of both their psyches. It would not work
out. He follows a rigid protocol.
Contradicting that man would be like facing
down the Church of God's prime minister.
Besides, she says she loves him. It's too hard-
hearted to go, so she decides to leave

it be. By night she studies till two, leafing
through *materia medica*, working
on her grasp of remedies. That's hardly
easy---the texts are vast. People call
on her to prescribe, to administer
first-aid, but that's not enough. She must face

herself. Tears pool and shimmer on her face.
Who in this noble parish could believe
her impasse---she who is so ministerial
in her office? Her tight mouth works,
her breathing shows she's seething like a cauldron,
not finding a way out of this hard

spot. Face it---she'd been trying to hold hard,
but she doesn't even leave a note. Call
the minister. The pills have done their work.

At the Bottom of Flint Hill Road

Even though it's been a mild winter,
and everything seems fine,
driving down Flint Hill Road,
there's a spot at the bottom
where the radio goes out,
and the 4-wheel drive
scatters the gravel.
A one-lane bridge,
the posts not holding.
The paving is gone, washed into the gully.

On each side, wilderness.
Thickets of bittersweet, greasewood,
prickly nettle, thistle, brier,
poke, spotted spurge, gorse,
chokeberry, bindweed, thorn.

A headless crone driving,
fettered in a burr coat.
A stench of terror about her---
an airless smell of lightless rot.
Goneness hollows her midriff---
yet---a weight, a hunger, an itch.
A black griffin claws into her shoulder.

She is caught in the undertow
of the unthinking river
where the road erodes
at the edge of the forest.

Acid shards, stones, broken edges,
scathe the snags and the shoals
in the channel of sludge
pulsing between the thickets
and the vastness of nothing.

Sandbags---sky-static---chase off
weasel, raccoon, possum, lizard,
beaver, snake, otter.

Pray that you never feel it.
The way is beyond here.
This daughter enlists
the mysteries of her art.
Purple geode in hand,
she wades into the water –
to know and to wash
the secret, fearful chambers of her heart.

Living Water

In winter, we can walk closer to the water.
Undergrowth that once blocked the way
flattens down and sifts into the ground.

At first, this January day felt like frozen iron,
but here at the stream, things are moving.

Deer have departed their nest.
Hardwoods bend in the breeze.

The stream flows on briskly
past a new high-water mark---not
dissolving the stones in its channel,
but washing them well.

The dark, clear stream is picking up speed.
Debris left from the drought
rides away from me swiftly---
A sudden scatter of gold leaves races by---
not saying good-bye---
not trying to explain.

The Perfect Setting

I don't know if it is me or my mother standing there,
set like a stone in a brooch.
It must be me because that is the set of my body,
my Lastex bathing suit, my hair-do.
I set about posing for the photographer,
carefully with my weight set on the supporting leg---
the other leg set gracefully, sans any weight at all,
so as to look thinner, not bulging at the thigh.
(Knowing how to stand does set one apart.)
I hold the towel out widely over my shoulders,
spreading it out with my hands like wings,
so as to set a wide top line to trick the eye
of a beholder into seeing a lady
with hanger shoulders, such as I don't have.

Thank goodness my hair is still set. Set and sprayed.
Here we are, pictured on the bench,
as I'll tell the social set back home.
My perfect children, obediently seated.
Our lunch set out.
A perfect set-up for the Ladies Home Journal.
We could be a stage set for a play about the ideal family.
See my handsome husband obediently cooking lunch?
Tonight at sunset we are set to dine
in one of the finer restaurants.
I have a list of all the nicest places.
We had the whole thing nicely set before we set out.
I hope the photographer appreciates
how nicely this scene is set. Me
posing – a perfect suburban housewife
vacationing in Florida with her darlings.
(I've had my heart set on this trip for quite a while.)
The table cloth so neatly set, the set of dishes matching,
nothing out of place.
Nothing pouring out of the beach bag.
I set value on such order.
The fruit set out on the plate just so.
The tidy picnic basket displaying silver flatware
set out in rows, held neat and tight by elastic straps.
No smoke from the cook-out fire.
No comments from the children, their faces set.

Sacrament

You haul me out of the dreamtime
by treading a tight circle about my head, counterclockwise.
I arise, refill your upstairs water,
clean, fresh, living water,
sprinkling in 3 drops of Flee Free,
the flower essence guaranteed to keep
you safe from darkling beings.

Now, down in the kitchen, we repeat
our inveterate, settled, morning domestic office,
me ministering to your prescribed needs.
You reverently attend the litany:
One hundred milligrams of Vitamin C;
One dose of Vetri-Science Nu-Cat, with Taurine;
a half-dropperful of White Willow Bark solution, sublingually;
Tapezol, sliced in half with the pill guillotine;
one-quarter Atenolol; one-eighth Vasotec---smithereens---really,
offered within a blob of Nutri-Cal.

Then, Feline Wysong Geriatrx Diet,
and, served in another vessel, Vitality Liver Gourmet,
sprinkled ceremoniously with Pro-Biotic.
In a third, clean Pyrex cup, pure water,
blessed with the flower essence.
No fair linen, but the elements presented on a pristine tray.

Take, eat.

We have survived the mysterious sufferings of that year
with ritual herbs: Foti, Hawthorn, Dandelion, Cornsilk;
the essences: Capeweed, Lemon, Lime, Calliandra, Vitex;
the rites of Hypericum, Aconite, Arnica,
Berberis, Phosphorous, Nux, offered on time, in potency.
Your illness was penance for? We do not know.
Your cure, miraculous, they say.
Is this expiation?

Once again, we observe our formal morning celebration
of yet another day, consecrated.
We have performed this communion,
it seems, forever and ever.

The sliding glass door opens.
You leap out into the day, sans absolution,
entering the kingdom of heaven.
Let your light so shine,
and keep the law for the time to come.

Invitation from a Dolphin

Come swim with us in our gorgeous ocean.
I'll introduce you to our calves.
Our babies' Moms always have a helper.
Their grandmothers can still nurse the babies, too.
You'll love our family.

I'll show you how to dive and leap skyward, whirling,
making dramatic, joyous splashes, and keep you safe
within our pod's field of energy---
A fabulous new healing experience for you.

We can talk, sing, blow big bubbles.
We'll examine you with echolocation clicks, creaks, squeals,
and heal any places that are slipping into negativity.

We are here to encourage you to communicate beyond your five senses.
We converse over long distances with special acoustics,
with signature whistles, seeking food, helping friends, navigating.
We have the ability to track the planets' magnetic fields
with surreal precision. Please do not interfere!

Noises disorient us. Please stop blasting seismic drilling.
It is as if all your smoke alarms go off at once,
and some giant tears into your home and bangs on your pots and pans,
while screaming to acid-rock recordings. Only worse.
This will make us crazy and will kill us.

We are related from way back--- the same family.
We offer answers to secrets you may not be ready to hear.
We hope you stop your barrage of fearful noise.
We hear things too well you cannot.
I wish you could hear me now.

Just a Tropic Shower

It is enough to array my bones on the silica shore,
Bones sprung from last night's undertow.
In this season of the hurricane,
The waves roll me underwater, then toss me onto the rainy strand.
The wet weight's still stuck within my ribs,
That same dead baby is rumbling in discontent.
Breasts overflowing with tides and stones,
Bursting ribs accept heat's fingers on their planes.
It is easy to say, in latitudes like this,
During the stormy season, oceanic feelings gust
With misplaced passions for the ephemeral present.
Easy to say it is just another tropical shower,
The sun out all the while, the end in sight,
No leaden three-day-blow that means to stay.
Still the final deluge of grieving
Detains me on this oasis island.
The staying-going welling up to overflowing.
Even the stasis of regrets and unknown knowings
Seems safer than the fearful letting-go.
The archipelago of ancient hours
Strings the sea with souvenirs.
Lagoons celled off by rings of reefs
Encircle secure atolls confining fortune's floods.
Beyond the reef, beyond the warm and yellow sand,
The open ocean lies, commanding:
Swim! Strike out and loose those shadow shapes---
Make for the open sea.

For Ellie

The day of the rain and the red wheelbarrow,
Ellie, the lady of the house, is away.
No one knows where she went, but it seems safe
for the gods of the garden to come out and to dance.

Gentle rain washes the kingdom clean
Deva creatures arrive to play
Raindrops drip music into baths for birds
Gray squirrels fly up and down
Meadow mice zip out of view
A box turtle steps left, steps right.

Lizards slither. A black snake, two toads love the wet
The King's Gold Cypress gives thought to her hair
Mallows (who might be Roses of Sharon) raise their faces
Pachysandra glitters---crepe myrtles, zinnias, sage,
hydrangea, azaleas preen in the mirror pools
rhodos, sedums, chives, mint
Leland Pines pretend they are on forest holiday.

Fairies twirl on the pine-needle floor.
Robin, finch, mocking bird, swallow, gull, woodpecker, hummer
shelter their feathers beneath the leaves.

The blue parasol thinks her thoughts
planning to write all of it down in time
Lanterns and baskets occupy the air.

Fragrances float in to ring the gongs and bells
vibrations sound as a sea breeze rises
inviting stacks of stones to restack themselves yet again.
Pebble paths lined with shells and standing figures
lead past glass spheres smiling steady on their pedestals
guiding to the secret shed where the clock has stopped at 5:30
Beetles, ants, butterflies stay hiding
Muses snooze. Spirits make free with illusions.

Sprites flicker and flutter four hands round.
Brownies, pixies, nymphs, gnomes sing their showery rainbow song
leaping into sky-high air turns,
flinging streamers of green light---
iridescent tourmaline, aventurine, malachite, emerald, jade.

Spatters, sprinkles slow. Voices tune up---
warbles, chirrs, trills, honks, chirps---
a symphony in off-beat unison.

The light changes
Creatures who know that they own the place
take liberties with mysteries---shadow, sun, rain---
and now shape-shift again, becoming airy nothings.

Edward gives his standing blessing, his eyes mirroring, protecting.

Treasure has been placed safely in the shed
The red wheelbarrow shows the way
Ellie comes home again
Her magic garden has resumed its usual gorgeous guise.

Green Lawn Gone

She saved
Her white gloves
From the days of
Grace and Jackie.
Back then, she wore her gloves
To dinner and the theater---
Traveling out in taxis.

Today, she wears her gloves
To cut the grass
That keeps on growing.
Whatever happens
(or fails to happen)
There's always mowing.

She wears her white gloves
Backed by Band-Aids,
To rake mowed grass
That had grown for days,
Then turned to hay,
And dried in silver wisps and lumps of greige.
Her gloves, her hair, her lawn
Have all gone gray.

Ghost Crab

You wouldn't even know it's there
until you see---or, rather, feel---
what seems to be a bit of sand---
-----scampering-----

And just as you have an inkling
it may not be sand,
it has vanished---
like a name, an idea, or a dream---
down deep into its unsounded hole.

Hindsigh

Shopping last summer,
I found a designer dress that was nearly irresistible.
It fit my figure, nipping here, flowing there, to flatter me.
Of silk knit, it was stylish, luxurious, bouncy, practical,
        eminently packable.
The background color set off my tan and pearls.
Its gorgeous print of blood-red roses tossed
        with dark green leaves broke my heart.
I desired the dress, but its exorbitant price deterred me.
Moreover, the dress was mute, not declaring,
"I am yours," as some have.

Now, in January,
I happen on the dress again, this time on sale,
        more affordable than before.
(Though surely I can have any item that speaks to me.)
I try on the dress. My tan has faded.
My figure (or the dress) has shifted.
A woman passerby glances my way and shakes her head, No!
That dress, so enravishing last season,
        is now a tawdry rag, which cannot be rejuvenated
        by being pressed, as the sales clerk is suggesting.

One summer, years ago,
I was captivated by a gentleman, who seemed irresistible.
His hands fit my figure, he flattered me.
He was bouncy, his background practical and stylish,
        implying luxury and travel.
With him, I felt desired.
The blood-red roses he brought me broke my heart.
At times a darker tone in his flowing conversation
        hinted I might have to pay a price I could not afford.
Besides, beneath it all, his voice was mute,
        not declaring, "I am yours," as some have.

Now at a museum opening,
I happen on that man again, this time with his new wife.
I observe them from a distance,
        and in the glass reflections of the art.
I see the woman resembles me as I was then.
How could this shrunken, shriveled man
        have ever attracted my attention?
He appears faded, a tawdry rag,
        never to be rejuvenated, even if I pressed
        as his shifting, suggestive smile requests.

Fog on Fowler Beach

Fog on all sides, just faintly breathing---
eclipsing familiar signs.
I'm here, unseeing.

A white-out. No horizon.
No heaven, no earth,
no shadow, no time.

Nothing is as it was before.
The tide is wildly low,
exposing an ancient,
otherworldly land.

An unnatural apparition---
a dark relic of some war---
a skewed black battlement
tilts---shrouded in the mist.

The low-tide odor of decomposition---
lives dissolving in the cold sand,
broken shells, scattered stones.
A few white feathers settle.

I might fear I've been
vaporized, dematerialized,
and stranded on some ghostly moon
with no sign to guide me.

But, eiderdown enwraps me.
A cushioning cloud is down around me,
swaddling all in unearthly muffling.
Tuning to seclusion,
we harmonize in peace.

Waves whisper in invisible surf.
A distant rocking, ringing buoy sounds its song.
A fog horn intones.....

home.....
        home.......
                home.....

Escorts on the Quest for Love

To me, those plants were just dusty touch-me-nots,
    rampant in the ravine,
But, Charles, the manchild who led me by the hand,
    proclaimed them to be---forget-me-nots!

Finally, we agreed with the field guide's name—jewelweed—
    gleaming beads glinting; exuberant seeds showering;
    green leaves that may heal.

Fleetingly, I feel I'm the wind, rippling the silver leaves'
    flowing mosaic,
    high in the embrace of the trees, on the peak of the hill.

But, the white birds kite away in unison, beyond my porch pillars,
    out of view, and I'm alone, again.

Tendrils of spent wild rambler roses invade my yard; their sharp barbs
    snag me as I go about my gardening.

Manfully, Charles tries to help me clear away the brambles, declaring,
    "I want to protect you! Let *me* cut them!"
But, he flails the blades perilously. Together, we'll learn
    from experience, how to handle the shears.

Heather serves me strawberries—luminous as rubies—
    sun-heated hearts
    she's hand-picked in the field.
I consume her fruits' splendid, temporal tenderness, but, then,
    only an ache and a stain on the plate remain for remembrance.
Looking for love, I find only rosy illusions. I can't give you
    the true jewels we seek, till I mine them myself.

Elfin Meg, intent on her mission, has slipped into my kitchen.
    I don't perceive her, tiny and silent, beneath my old table.
Attentive, adoring, pinafored in pink, she patiently waits,
    determined to nurture my kitten.
I'm abashed, when at last, I discover her.
    Caring love blooms in its own time—
    evasive, elusive, enduring as truth.

Everything Is Gold

Today, everything is gold.

The lemon slice in my ice water………gold.
My bowl of yellow tomato gazpacho………gold.
My Mimosa, cold in its chilled flute.........gold.
Black-eyed susans, zinnias, yarrow, marigolds......... gold.
Tassels blowing atop the corn fields.........swirls of gold.
Glancing froth on the ocean swells……… shimmering gold.
Fluffy, slow-floating clouds sailing on ……… fringed with gold.
The blazing sun………shedding gold.

The light between you and me drenches us in gold.
Now I'm old, everything is gold.

Dry Dock

Your flags snapped at the halyard
Signing: Come aboard.
Still, no pipes played.

Half my barefoot weight
Pressed your deck away
Causing a straddle of split suspension.

Ballasted with sleep like pig-iron,
Your bulkhead slipped away,
Widening the stripe of rivening water.

But still your craft remains
Tied fore and aft
By uneasy hawsers.

Close

The light that I shall see when I die
Resides in teal-gray horizon waves
Ignited by the sun within the wind cloud
Where particles of poems fly
Closing in on the secret. Then
The mercury breaks
And I'm left with silver pieces once again.

Dogwood

Layers of white butterflies
Weave new tablecoths,
Lying out in flat folds
Stretched taut to dry,
Pinned on vertical thorns,
Caught in the dark wood,
Wafers of horizon

Censing

Deadheading petunias
of a summer night,
etherized in their
ruffled sweetish reek
of bitter face-powder, touch of clove
fuzzy crumpled
parasols stick
to my fingertips

Was that you
in the garden
that night?
Paper lanterns
dappled by blackening
leaves, distant music,
drum line insistent

an odor floating like smoke
from a joss stick,
or a pastille,
a bit of civet,
a bite of ginger, citrus
a cirrus of nicotiana
and petunias
surprising the shadows

Tonight, the screech owl warbles,
something moves
in the lamplight glancing
the rhododendron,
the inkling of black pine

I glimpse you moving
away again in the mist
the slant of your shoulder,
your narrow head tilting.
Will you turn around,
lift your eyebrow, and look at me
one last time?

Broken Connection

"Daedalus?" What does that strange word mean?
You demand, suspicious by long-distance.
Your myths are different, your kind of climbing---
After all, flying fathers,
Christian martyrs, young artists,
Are not juicy doings or chewable news
To show off at country club luncheons.

Icarus, at least, got wings from his dad,
Who, at least, flew safely to Sicily.
At last, I'm underway on my course
Propelled by the sun to dragon-filled seas.
So, best tell your friends in the box and the maid
That I'm taking a tour
Through some alien isles
Where the ship-to-shore's broken
And another language is spoken.

Bougainvillea

Hot-pink papery bouquets
airy sprays of flame-fuschia
tissue-paper bits,
ruffled, weightless,
like display stuff, decoration,

splay on dainty
sun-tanned stalks. Some
rigid twigs poke the air, one
sprig is abruptly broken, dead, yet
the stems are mainly lively tendrils,
viney, with lime-green
faintly heart-shaped leaves
concealing thorns.

The true blooms of the bougainvillea
are inconspicuous amid this fiesta
of sultry magenta incandescence.
Three vivid, crisp, lightly veined translucent coin-shaped bracts
surround and clasp three central, furled
petaline purple spires,
which bear the flowerets.
Tiny modest chalk-white
five-pointed asterisks
burst from beaded tips—
miniscule white stars of dry ice, edged in pink—
Snow sparks prevailing over fire.

What would Louis Antoine de Bougainville think to see
this alien beauty boxed in on a back deck here in West Grove?
Displaced from a pergola in Greece,
Lately seen in Martinique, Belize,
a flash of sensation flares.
Something ravishing, painted lips of passion,
which may hide teeth or even razor blades.
Something of soft escape to the fabled faraway—
drums, ankle bells, the hot black jungle. The lure
of a conch shell horn calling over blue Bahamian seas.
Something of wild seduction,
A second's frisson, the suffering sure to follow.

A Lesson

The edge of the diving board
skinymarinky me—jittering
up to yet another leap
in a long afternoon of leaps
into the black-tea lake
when some smart-alecky boys
dare me to shed my kapok life-preserver
see if I can paddle to the raft on my own
Smarty pants I fling it
heavy wet onto the splintery dock
I yell Easy!
Show-offy saucy
I leap
bubbles light beneath
just me and the lake
something private
it was even easier
my unpillowed middle told me
The water would always hold me up

Air Turns

Yes!
Even at my age,
I was dancing on the beach!

At 4 p.m.
the iridescent shallows
were sky.

A distant fisherman
was oblivious to
my run, run, run leaps---and

to the invisible silver line
clasped at my breastbone---
looping my tour jetés higher.

Then, a precocious Yorkshire terrier---
perceiving my glee---came running
like a battery toy from behind some pilings.

Engaging my eye, he flew
into a four-legged spin---
a dizzy and fringed propeller---

showing his appreciation for my expertise
by duplicating it in his own style---
awaiting my doubled delight and applause.

Like exalted fountain spouts,
we alternated our variations on joy,
and then he bowed away, over the sand.

Amazing Lace

My mind is intricate, stylish, old-fashioned lace.
My mind retains archaic French vocabulary:
"La laset"---lace, a snare, a trap---
"lacher"---to loose, to let slip from the net.

The net of my lacey mind practices catch and release.
I caught your name; then let it go free.
Lyrics of old Broadway show tunes replay perfectly in my mind,
including the scratches on the 33.
But, what-all I was to buy at the store has escaped
to wherever lists vanish to.

The design of the lace that is my mind is singular---
unlike any other pattern.
But years ago, meaning well,
they tried to reembroider, overlayer
my original, wild work of art.

The layers that they ordered have since unraveled.
New perforations have appeared---
open spaces---keyholes, windows.
My mind remains a type of seine,
private lacework, catching and releasing.
Careful cutwork, ancient, mended, transformed
to lace revised---my friend and loose adornment---
rich and strange.

Lacuna

Rich kids gobble up
hot dogs at the Cape Cod Yacht Club
up there where white sails
skim perfect blue waves
in the clear sun,
while I'm stuck
here in these parched fields,
as fountains and wells go dry.

This must be a lacuna—
a mere time of waiting on hold
till the barbed wire of pain
will eventually consent to let go.

A moth's body on the stair
looks dark, dusty, and dead—yet
when I try to pick it up,
it flies away lightly—
an example of what rises—
such as the elevator
that opens precisely on time—
such as groundwater,
such as perilous hope.

Ada's Exit

I'm riding up the New Jersey Turnpike
in fading November light:
The sign Montclair
arises, dies—
I speed on by.

Time was, I'd get off there.
A few trips it took
for me to be easy with
right-left-left directions
to arrive at Ada's place,
fresh-cut red celosia in my hand,
that I'd picked up at a roadside stand.

What do we call that mutilating breach—
when flowers freeze
and a certain essence leaves?

Early April Loves

When lingering winter's grip feels grim and unremitting,
Stark, isolated shadow shapes mark faded yards and fields.
Dark stalks and wiry branches cower, brittle with the cold.
Then, like shimmering streams of fireflies, gleaming in the night,
Forsythia fountains cascade, spilling light in dim, forgotten places.
I love those bright, reviving, radiant beacons!
Flowering golden sprays of life gently bend, lift my sight.
Graceful spires of hope open to the April rain.

Sheltering banks that range the length of April's rolling field embrace
A shimmering creek, flowing deep within the dark ravine.
Protective willows, withered weeds, wild roses overgrow
The baby river, rising cool, clean, clear.
I love that stream of gleaming, living water!
The steady current pours from its source, the spring,
Follows its course, washing rocks and obstacles,
Sweeping, spilling, swelling, impelled to the distant, open sea.

She ranges home again from yards and fields,
Or, from the creek, where eagerness and instinct lure her.
Wriggling, shaking, spraying water, she tenders gifts,
Forsythia twigs, with spills of yellow kisses
Gracing her dampened cheeks.
Golden retriever blood impels my vibrant puppy,
Still, I believe the source that nurtures her is love.
I love that joyful, wet, and flowery furry courier!
Her adoring, open smile sweeps like a radiant beacon of gleaming light.

Blood on Our Hands

Our yard is awash in blood. A female baleen whale and her calf lie dead on tarps, their bodies awaiting necropsies. We wheel out our stainless-steel table--- with a drainage hole at one end. We assemble our collection of butcher knives, carving knives, #10 blades, calipers, measuring rods, clip boards, forms, pens that work, surgery tools, bags, labels, the camera, buckets, trash cans, hoses. We sharpen our knives. We stagger in heavy plastic coveralls, hoods, masks, double gloves, boots in the August heat. We stand in blood. We are near the sea, but its breeze does little to cool us nor to blow away the stench. Ellie runs to the hospital to beg more #10 blades. We are volunteers. I, the scribe, stand by to take notes: All day and most of the night, we observe, cut, measure, bag, call out, write: weight of kidneys, stomach contents, number of teeth present (if not baleen), condition of lungs and liver, lacerations, scars, predation, parasites. Nothing about the missing whale song.

We find a spray-can cap lodged in the mother's digestive tract. It killed the whale and her baby. Starved to death. We are losing what is beautiful. We have blood on our hands.

Balance Point

Creek leaves lie on the line
Between water and air.
Gaze in the wet windows,
Patterns plastered on panes.
Tickets, stubs, leavings
Of last summer,
Floating, reflecting
The last light of April.
Clean currents flow cold
Under the leaf-skin.
Sunshine sifts through new tree leaves
Into that glimmering disc---
That wet healing laser.

Books Are History

There were no books at home.
When I was ten or so, I'd walk up the hill, past Clifton School,
    then board the street car to ride
    to The Corryville Public Library for the day.
I took my sandwich in a paper bag
    and ate it at noon with a 5-cent orange drink.

The library was quiet and knew everything.
So did the ageless librarian, beneath her topknot.
She taught me the Dewey Decimal System and showed me the stacks.
I knew I had found my true home.

Married at 18, living in a college town,
I spent my days in the archives,
    reading my way straight down the shelves, author by author.

When my husband disappeared into the Navy with our only car,
I ordered books by mail----especially classics----
    with leather-like bindings and "gold" trim.
No matter where we had to move,
    my books kept me company and made me feel safe.

Divorced and finally starting university in my forties,
I'd lug laundry baskets to the college library to fill up
    with enough books sufficient
    for the makings of a good grade.

Eventually, my walls were lined with all kinds of books---
    fiction, hard backs, geographies, hand books, translations,
    soft covers, anthologies, grammars, novels, poetry, manuals,
    encyclopedias, field guides, dictionaries, biographies, Cassell's,
    Roget's, signed first editions, Bartlett's, *Materia Medica*,
    collections, histories.
They served as buffers---insulating me from the world.

Then, I landed my dream job. I was paid to read books!
Publishers would send me copies of whatever I desired.
I'd read all day at work---sometimes outside under a tree—
Back home again, with my cup of soup, I'd read the night away.

Finally, as I was old, they told me I needed a tiny condo.
I had to let go of some of my things---especially my books---
        my beloveds, my friends, my protectors.
The Book Barn offered me store credit, but all I wanted to buy
        from that place was my own books back.

Today, somewhere, an occasional store still sells books—
        ----calendars, toys, games, greeting cards, and gifts.
Too few sanctuaries remain for old volumes
        from estates of a by-gone era.
These treasures are valuable for collectors.
Millennials must consider them mere old-fashioned trash---
        used---and, alas, disintegrating.
Where shall I go to wander amid the dusty stacks
        of such a book refuge,
        listening for a book to call my name?

These days, people believe they are reading books
        when they hold up their Kindles,
        or whatever they call those devices.
Not me---I want a real bound book to cradle in my hands.
I need to use my fingers to turn the page, to turn it back, to mark it up.
Then to place the book back on the shelf to join its fellows,
        where they will continue to transmit wisdom and understanding--
        even as I sleep---where they will continue to keep me safe.

Traveling to the Chicken-Dinner Place:
The Tragedy of the Corn Fritter

"Hotter than blazes," according to my father.
Summertime in old Cincinnati. No A/C.
 "It's not the heat, it's the humidity," we tell each other.
Piling into the black Chevy, we flee the concrete city,
riding over the Ohio River, exhaling the dying day----
The sun letting down its bloody yolk, its ball of heat---
behind sweeping fields of Kentucky corn.
Relief. We breathe again.

The green sea parts as we roll long the road---
last light gilding the emerald corridors of corn---
gold-tinged oceanic fields rustling in the summer wind.

First stop---Clutters' Farm.
Cows calling, ambling home---
pigs lounging in muddy puddles---
barnyard odors---dung, musk---
Big bales of new-mown hay.
Fragrance of summer sun from crazy tomatoes,
exuding heat, lush on vines.
True peaches, watermelons, honest squash,
real-life blue berries in cardboard boxes,
and, of course------corn.   We load up.

On to the chicken-dinner place---
A square, screened-in pavilion
with a ceiling of stamped tin tiles
sheltering long tables covered in checkered oil cloth---
Daisies, black-eyed susans, goldenrod in Mason jars.
No menus. Benches. We take our places.

Substantial, smiling farm women in flowered frocks
and non-matching print aprons
bring our feast: country chicken, freshly fried in molten lard---
cousins of those lively birds still pecking in the yard.
Bowls of chard with bacon fat, mashed potatoes, skillet gravy,
snap beans with ham, sliced tomatoes---
baskets of biscuits. Pitchers of farm honey---
fresh bread just out of the wood stove, butter (compliments of cows),
and corn fritters. Luscious corn fritters.

Farm daughters in short shorts, pigtails bouncing,
bring each of us a single, solitary corn fritter.
Only one corn fritter.
A fritter the size of a Cincinnati Reds baseball---
Bronze on the outside---crispy to bite into.
Inside the bite---cake-like, straw-yellow ambrosia
studded with corn kernels from ears
hand-picked less than an hour ago---
out there in the Elysian field just beyond the screen.
Each fritter sits in its own saucer of viscous syrup.
Oh, my!

I do not think to ask for another.
Neither does my brother.
We fail to ask for more!
Tragedy. Catastrophe. Disaster.
All my attempts at recipes have been fiascos.

Seventy-some years have passed
sans a single corn fritter.
I am old, dismayed, stricken.
It is too late to retrace the way
to that long-gone,
(probably a strip-mall now),
vanished, enchanted chicken-dinner place.

To Whom It May Concern:

No need for your concern.
This is just to say
I am no longer whoever you may have thought I was.
My costume remains the same---the casual uniform
Of my group---all retired---but they are young and new.

For my new title, I pick Cabbage.
Or, better, the light part of the froth atop an ocean wave.
My right hand is reaching for the next rung up
as my sole falters trying to gain new footing.

No need for you to assess my haircut, nor my shoes.
All that has fallen away.
Well, some of it, anyway.
This is just to say, I am no longer the old me.
This older me is new, or newish---more knowing, seasoned.
Also shriveled, dwindling, airy, vanishing, ghostlike, frail.
My bag is packed.   One foot is out the door.
I try to find my way.

You may see for yourself if any of this seems true.
We can have lunch, if you want.
I'd like to hear your news---how life is treating you.

Love, Elisabeth

Time Travel

We're resting from floating
in the salt bay off Broadkill Beach.

A hot shower melts me.
I ease into an ancient wicker chair
facing the marsh
and the silver river flowing beyond.

A shift. As the sun slants orange
through the glinting sea of grass---
A pine branch overhead frames the scene.

A silent beast rises up with a splash
and lumbers away into the dusk.

Time Being

While I sit here making simple rhyme,
the rest of the world is stressed
for lack of time.
They all run madly here and there,
As I did once. How come
I now have so much time and they so little?
My past six years compressed
would fit into a fiddle.

How does it appear from outer space –
All their rushing, while I remain in place?
Are clocks out there different?
Is a jiffy riffed by a trumpet call?
Do we live in no time after all?

Time and Again: Sasega Island

Massenet's "Meditation"
Flows ralletando, ritenuto,
Smoothing the lake in easy measures.
Yellow pond lilies, waving sedges
Fringe the island deep in pines.
Beyond Muskoka, Moose Deer Marina,
Out in the open, the Carolines.
A blue-jeaned blond boy
Repeats his flute songs
Where Ojibway pipes blew peace,
A fugue of races and generations.

Nighttime water conducts glissandos
Fluid through rushes, channeling sounds.
Flute lines, owls, curlews fly
Over deep-toned boulders, Ontario's ages.

Mosses and lichens scale the stones
Where few canoes go whistling through
That blue-green passage of music and water,

Called by the Indians: Ugo Igo.

The Train

At night, in bed, I feel the train rocking me.
It cries out, "whooo—oo—eee"
    as it clickety-clacks down the railroad track.

Where is this train going?
Can it be the same train I heard in Stuart,
    as I lay on my canvas army cot,
    back when we had black-out shades to keep us safe?

The snow was deep in Ohio.
The Salvage Corps arrived to take us
    to Cincinnati's Union Station---
    mosaics on the massive walls---
    planes, trains, steamboats, Model Ts.
A man with a microphone asked us,
"Are you arriving or leaving?"
We were on the radio---WKRC!

Down the black staircase we went---down to the stony depths.
The train, like some sort of animal straining to be loose,
    awaited, steaming.
We found our car.
The conductor held my hand as I stepped up on the stool he had placed.
I was aboard.

We lurched forward, banged back, forward again---
    and we were rolling.
Slowly, at first.
The whistle blew.
Outside, in the cold, people on the platform moved backwards.
Inside, in comfort, we traveled forward.

I pinched the shade down and took off my nasty snowsuit---
    itchy, scratchy, unlined, almost-black wool.
The porter came---a kindly magician---
    who, with sleight-of-hand, converted my seat into a bed
    with crisp white sheets and a tan blanket that smelled of smoke.
Coal dust powdered the window sill.
A net hammock swung at the end---it was meant to hold my shoes.

Tucked in, I pinched the shade back up.
From my darkened berth, unseen, I watched the world go by.
First, city windows---I looked inside lighted kitchens, bedrooms---
    seeing the lives of people I'd never know.
The train took over, rocking me.
I was asleep.

Soon awake, peeking out, I saw the backyards of Georgia.
Swamplands, shacks, fires where people were cooking.
The train was a snake of cars.
From my Pullman window, I could see our engine way ahead,
    pulling us around a distant bend.
The coal car followed the engine.
A big man in an undershirt shoveled coal into the raging hell-fire
    that powered us forward.

Breakfast was served in the dining car.
Starched white napery and heavy flatware.
The waiter called me Missy and declared that the trout he served me
    had just been caught at the last water stop.

I explored an observation car, passenger cars, a club car, freight cars.
Finally the caboose.
Moving between cars was scary.
The loose metal connections thrashed wildly.
I could see the rocky roadbed flash by beneath my feet.
The door to the next car was heavy and hard to open.

Then---orange trees!
I ran to both sides of our car as we rolled through a tunnel of
    orange groves fragrant with white blossoms and fat fruit
    glistening in the warm sun.
I put on my yellow dotted-swiss sunsuit.

The train lurched to a stop.
Cars banged together.
Holding the conductor's hand, I stepped down onto the sand.
Palm trees. A new place.

There were more trains to come---
To Syracuse, to towns out west---to Villefranche, Naples, Rome.
Always alone---especially when not alone.
As I shall be tonight, rocked by the train traveling down the track.
Clickety-clack, clickety-clack, whooo-oo-eee!

Trying the Ice

Strobe sun
Bounces on noon
Snow. Green eyes flash.
Who can see?
Angora aura
Feathers the ginger air
Brushing intimations of vision
Eider-down insulates,
Gift-wrapped cushions,
White as a bride.
Black moves the crystallized creek,
Watching with one eye,
The consent of one circle of snow.
Unroll the white wedding carpet,
Ribboning the path.
Who will walk?
Ice-mirrors shine heart-shaped.
Tip-toe marks of a doe
A dainty dice-toss of toe-nails
Scatters aslant this snow creek,
Till now, an untouched silk streamer,
Flicked at each end,
Flashing the surface to skim,
Where otter, that tentative heart,
Warily navigates the water.

Uneven Footing

This path I trek today—
up and down, with sudden turns—
has roots like giant hands
or claws—reaching across the slanting ground.

Roots exposed, lying on the surface—
prominent and plain to see—
resembling twisted innards.

Wiry roots might span a ditch
covered with fallen leaves—wet and smelling rank—
knotty, garbled roots, illegible, concealed, unseen.
I must keep looking down as I go, lest I fall.

But, stop! Here is a red post marker, Number 9,
a few feet away from this steady, tall white oak
with its accommodating several trunks
opening to me like arms.
A listening tree.

I take a seat inside it. A breathing space.
Now, pause. Look up—higher than that soaring hawk
and out beyond this little, transitory woods.

Here's an intermission.
Shift, suspend inside this inland sea.

What Goes Round

My sock came back.
A very old sock.
I got it years ago when I bought
A sweatsuit at the outlet—
Pleased at the match,
Both socks and suit the same violet blue.

Over the years, each piece
Faded at the same rate.
Life changed, the job ceased.
So, I wear my comfy, fleecy
P.J.-sort-of-outfit nearly daily.
It has become my second skin,
Molding to my rounded shoulders, knobby knees,
It is me—and easy.

Then one evening,
I left one faded violet sock outside my locker.
When I came back, the sock was gone—evaporated.
Nor was it in the lost-and-found.

Head said fret not.
Your sock drawer overflows.
The sweatsuit's old, too, and holey.
Discard it—all.
Shed that skin, it's evolution.
But heart felt her hollow.
Besides, when a single sock goes missing,
Something's loose in the universe,
And unease follows.

Then, last night, on the floor,
Outside the locker, lay my sock!
Crumpled from its travails—
But my own sock, with its familiar thready edge,
Its odd, washed-out hue.
My sock lay sprawled out in full view.
Come to Mama!

Now, back home again,
Washed and reunited with its mate,
The stray lies curled up and safe
Amid its brighter, newer fellows.
The lost is found, the world is round,
The universe is ordered, after all.

Sock Happy

I believe in joy.
Therefore, I have locked up my grumpy black socks
(irreversibly flocked with sullen, stubborn dryer lint).
I never want to see black socks again.

My bright new socks live in a willow basket,
each pair rolled into the shape of an Easter egg,
suggesting renascence, renewal.
My socks cuddle together lovingly,
singing merry high-pitched sock songs in three-part harmony---
giggling when they see me approach.

Vivid, smiling, sunshiny socks!
Every color, hue, tone, shade you have ever heard of, plus new ones:
verona, putty, copper, graphite, pomegranate, flax, light potato, lotus.
They come in stripes, prints of flowers, leopard's spots, stars,
paisley, chevrons, footprints, argyles, polka dots.

For more fun, layer your legs:
tights or leggings colored purple prose go on first.
Next, pull up knee-highs---different Technicolor looks for each leg---
Finally, the finale, unmatching witty, jazzy anklets.
It doesn't matter what else you wear,
but hanging a sheer vermillion scarf with knotted fringe can't hurt.

You'll hear the drums and trumpets sound
and find yourself dancing the KiKi all the way to joy.

A wise woman says: "It's true:
Adorn your legs and you will
adore all the joy they lead you to."

My Flare

Fairy lights, like fireflies,
bring a gentle, magic glow to our lives.

When a single, stringed star nears its end,
it flares--sparkler-like---
a heightened kaleidoscope of life.
Then it dies.

These days, I live in such a light.
All the marbles roll my way:

The waiter from Jamaica asks permission---
then (on my cheek) he kisses me!

Strangers on the street smile and wave.
(Perhaps they mistake my grimace for a greeting.)

A shopkeeper pops out,
hands me a long-stemmed rose.

Daughterly girls offer their info, promising
they will gladly pitch in if I need assistance.

I tell you, this is joy!

You say, Stop! Enough !
Too extravagantly Pollyana.
There needs to be a break here, a reversal,
for the sakes of art and truth.

Sorry, no can do.
I'm not in the mood.
I am a flaming daylily, loving my flare.

All right, it's true.
There may be a bit of pain.
I stagger, stumble, drop my cane.
Strong arms show up from out of nowhere.
I'm airborne, transported
safe and charmed to the other side.

Lunching on the wharf---
petunias blooming, flags flying in the ocean breeze.
Here's a glass of Chardonnay, on the house.
It's a glorious, beautiful day.
Too beautiful, you might say.

I believe I hear a waltz.
Could that be the King of Siam, bowing, offering his hand?
Shall we dance?

Going Home on the Coastal Highway

I'm on my way home, closer now---riding along the Coastal Highway.
Tourist season is in a welcome lull.
Air is cooler, crystalline, as Toni likes it.   We see ahead clearly.
It's late in Indian summer. Fall is coming down. Before long---winter.

During high summer, a land-locked skiff rocked
     on the emerald waves of a lively corn field, roadside.
The green stalks have turned brown;
     the grain got chopped off for the animals.
Now the boat is stuck in the stubble.

I drive on. A drowsy fly buzzes against the windshield,
     seeking freedom.
Geese fly in formation overhead---the young practicing for their trip.
Owls call for their mates. Maybe a snowy owl if we are lucky.

At a road-side stand, a mile-long line of pumpkins makes a chain
     where sunflowers and zinnias
     recently held their flashy fashion parade.
Summer corn and peaches are over, yet melon samples still are free.
Apples are in.   The cider is fresh---so make time to stop.
Mums, plums, herbs, rhubarb, jams, yams, beans, cabbage, honey.
Snap and bob to the country music playing on their radio.

I turn off at 13 Curves Road----not ready for home yet.
Maybe a chance to spot Carla looking for marsh hawks.
Soon Julie will be patrolling Broadkill by moonlight
     checking for migrants---we expect a seal or two---
     overnight guests resting on the beach.

Hurricane season is over.
I am having too much fun to go home.
     I'll put on my new Dardo dress, purple cape,
      and quite a few strings of beads, scarves, and shawls in crazy
      prints of genius colors: competition for the goldenrod, iron weed,
      loosestrife, poke--- clouds of swallowtail, and monarchs.
I'll ride down to the Boardwalk and from my perch in Victoria's,
     keep watch over the infinite ocean.
I might even see a mermaid.

Snow Day 1

No place to go day
Sheltering safely inside day
Looking inside my mind day
Cleaning out a drawer or cupboard day
Clearing away day
Taking a nap while awake day
Practicing dying day

Snow Day 2

Insulated in the privacy of silence
The outside world muffled in a white hush
My inside world---the middle of my mind---practicing peace
On the table, a bronze urn of flowering forsythia branches
Blooming in a wild snowstorm of baby's breath grounded with juniper
The outside world at a standstill, except for the wind chimes
Inside becomes outside---monastic serenity descends
Starry flakes make a meditation in the white quiet
Transforming my world into a serene dreamscape
Magical, mysterious, chaste, alive in a sacred sleep
Out in the field, snow geese pave the land covered in unending snow
In one breath the geese arc up into the boundless sky
Joining the snow---as do I---feather, flake, infinite me---all together
Becoming heaven

Surrender

Thanks be for the blessings of fatigue.
Gravity pulls decision to the ground.
Any drive toward enterprise is vain.

No will to thrash against the constant now.
Debility gives leave to simply be
And rest in level acquiescence of the heart.

Floating

Late afternoon, early fall---
blue sky, scattered clouds---
barefoot, over the sand I go---
test with my toes, then I step
into the still-warm, lapping water
at the place our bay
becomes the open ocean.

Out over the washboard bottom---
farther out---deeper, deeper I go--
then----a lift.

Knees rise, waterborne.
Shoulders let slip the day, the years.
Awash in the salt sea,
I loaf and lean into my life ring.

All falls away.

A shift.
Flesh becomes emptiness.
I drift in the water-sky---
pulled by the white moon,
guided by the current,
dissolved in the tide.

My Scars

I like to show my scars.
I flash my thigh---
the reddish railroad tracks
from knee to hip---
they never fail to get a rise:

First comes the wince of horror---
followed quickly by the balmy,
"Isn't it amazing what they can do these days…"
as if you could have your head removed,
and soon you'd be all right----
perhaps improved.

Some scars I do not show, you know.
They hide---buried in the dark---
quite apart---where they cannot bite.
Secrets that seek asylum
deep inside my mid-section,
my lizard brain, my heart.

My Beach

I stand here on what I call my beach.
At my back---salt-marsh odors of gentle disintegration---
and all that I leave behind.

I have looked my last, or nearly last,
on a life I'd never dreamed I'd leave---
Now, it is almost time.

Standing barefoot on this sand, I face the sea.
For me, this beach is the dividing line
between then---and soon---a fresh new life for me.

For now, I'm stuck on the cusp of summer ending and early fall.
The doldrums: too-heavy air, a stationary front,
still water, no current, dead low slack tide---poised---

in the pregnant pause that holds fertile possibilities---
from sudden vanishings to exciting surprise hellos.
These arise when the tide turns noisily to flood.

I might have died! I like to show my scars.
See here---on my beach and on me---a scraggly wrack line---
Well short of the dune despite the last full moon.

Parts of a loggerhead washed in (a propeller brought his end);
a dead terrapin and a carcass too far-gone to name.
I love best the broken whelk shells with cut-out walls---

elegant architecture---so freely released---
translucent crab molts, sharks' teeth, dried egg cases---
perhaps a prehistoric bone, a family of fossils

left from ancient bygone trials at civilizations. One worn coin,
jeweled sea-glass shards---pounded, polished, abraded---
tumbled with stones and sand in the open ocean.

My friends---my tribe---we plan a monster bonfire on this beach
to incinerate constrictions we no longer need. We invite
the stars to look down upon our sacred ceremony and to smile.

I do know about the undertow, rip currents, and perhaps a stumble
into an unexpected hole: the sandy suction in the surf
could pull my feet out from under me, testing my resolve.

I've heard that during an offshore hurricane
a towering wave might rise, smash against the shore,
and crash over one who stands naively on the beach---

dragging the innocent out to sea---to her wild demise.
Stings from rays and jelly fish, bites from stranded seals---
in glare and chop it is not possible to clearly see.

This salt air heals me. A pod of dolphins leaps.
An icy reviving spirit slices out of the breaking waves.
I receive myself.

I shall always remember what the light is like today,
as I step seaward toward the rolling sweep---
breathing in vitality from the oceanic deep.

Behind me lies what I once believed I'd understood.
I enter this vast unfathomable silent sounding---
this new life that I have almost found.

This beach, this sand, this edge on which I stand
is holy ground.

Under

Under laughter, sobs;
Under doubt, knowledge;
Under fear, the rock;
Under hurry, eternity.

About the Poet

 Elisabeth Stoner has benefitted by associations with many poets:

She has received charming notes from Robert Bly and Agha Shahid Ali. Shahid edited Wesleyan University's collection of ghazals.

Elisabeth enjoyed a drink with Elizabeth Bishop and spent a weekend with Allen Ginsberg doing "Snapshot Poetics" at the Zen Mountain Monastery in upstate New York.

Peter Matthiessen said he liked her poetry because it was honest. She was kissed by Howard Nemerov after lunch at a club in Philadelphia. She has studied with Gibbons Ruark, W.D. Snodgrass, Elise Paschen, Jeanne Murray Walker, Fleda Brown, and more recently, Ethan Joella, Gail Cormorat, and Elizabeth Dolan.